NORTHERN PACIFIC RAILWAY

D1567370

John Kelly

Iconografix
PHOTO ARCHIVE SERIES

Iconografix
PO Box 446
Hudson, Wisconsin 54016 USA

Library of Congress Control Number: 2007920338

ISBN-13: 978-1-58388-186-6
ISBN-10: 1-58388-186-7

07 08 09 10 11 12 6 5 4 3 2 1

Printed in China

Cover and book design by Dan Perry

Copyediting by Suzie Helberg

Cover caption:
Northern Pacific's North Coast Limited crossing the Continental Divide in the Western Montana Rockies. *JM Gruber collection*

BOOK PROPOSALS

Iconografix is a publishing company specializing in books for transportation enthusiasts. We publish in a number of different areas, including Automobiles, Auto Racing, Buses, Construction Equipment, Emergency Equipment, Farming Equipment, Railroads & Trucks. The Iconografix imprint is constantly growing and expanding into new subject areas.

Authors, editors, and knowledgeable enthusiasts in the field of transportation history are invited to contact the Editorial Department at Iconografix, Inc., PO Box 446, Hudson, WI 54016.

www.iconografixinc.com

Table of Contents:

Acknowledgements

Special thanks to J.M. Gruber (Mainline Photos) for help with this book and access to his collection of scenic Northern Pacific Railway photographs. Friends Bill Raia, Bruce Meyer, Doug Wornom, and John Pedersen also shared their photo collections. Coi Drummond-Gehrig of the Denver Public Library—Western History Collection was most helpful. Thank you to my partner Linda Shult for her proofreading skills and the Iconografix staff for publishing this book.

My memories of the Northern Pacific go back to 1960 when my dad took me to St. Paul Union Depot for Saturday train watching. The Depot was grand, built in the neo-classical style with 10 commanding pillars guarding the front entrance at Fourth and Sibley streets in downtown St. Paul. In their heyday, passenger trains from nine railroads served St. Paul Union Depot. Inside, the magnificent waiting room had a large skylight, brass ticket-wickets, a restaurant, gift shop, and bowling alley. The large train arrival-departure board separated the waiting area from the concourse. I remember standing by the windows, looking at the tracks below. Yard engines were busy switching coaches and sleepers as mail cars were being loaded, but one train always stood out above the others. The train was led by Electro-Motive diesel locomotives followed by spotless coaches in two-tone green with a white band. Car attendants greeted passengers boarding the train, and soon you could hear the conductor shout the "all aboard" call for the Vista-Dome North Coast Limited to the Pacific Northwest.

John Kelly
Madison, Wisconsin
August 7, 2006

Introduction

The story of the Northern Pacific Railway, the first of the northern transcontinentals, is the saga of adventure and discovery in the Pacific Northwest. On July 2, 1864, the nation's 16th president, Abraham Lincoln, signed an Act of Congress creating the Northern Pacific Railway. The railroad stretched 2,000 miles from Minnesota's Lake Region, over the broad prairies of North Dakota and Montana's magnificent Rockies, past Idaho's lakes and forests to Puget Sound and the great seaports of Seattle-Tacoma and Portland. The mainline closely followed the route blazed in 1804 by Captains Meriwether Lewis and William Clark, foremost of America's inland explorers. The railroad survived the Great Panic of 1873 and the failure of Jay Cooke, the company's banker. As the route west continued to be built, 15,000 Chinese laborers and 10,000 Americans worked from opposite ends of the line until the last spike was driven September 8, 1883, at Gold Creek, Montana, in a ceremony attended by General Ulysses S. Grant and Henry Villard, the Northern Pacific's vibrant president.

In 1893, while visiting the Chicago World's Fair, NP chief engineer E.H. McHenry saw a Korean flag bearing the Tai Chi symbol of yin and yang—opposites that together define a whole. McHenry introduced the Monad symbol to the Northern Pacific and it was soon used on passenger cars, rolling stock, stations, and public timetables. NP viewed the Monad as a symbol of good luck and good transportation for its passengers.

Always a leader in progressive railroading, Northern Pacific was the first road to offer sleeping and dining car service from St. Paul to the Pacific Northwest. Following its inauguration on August 29, 1900, the railroad's flagship North Coast Limited consistently ranked among the finest passenger trains in North America. It was upgraded in 1930 with radio music, showers, and a barbershop. In September 1948 the North Coast Limited entered the streamlined era with six sets of lightweight, Pullman-Standard-built coaches, diners, and lounge cars painted in a two-tone, dark olive green with gold striping.

Committed to offering the best in deluxe passenger service, on November 15, 1952, the North Coast Limited was upgraded with a striking new two-tone green livery bestowed by industrial designer Raymond Loewy. The colors mirrored the lush shades of the train's Pacific Northwest terminus and displayed the NP Monad logo in the center of each car just below the window line. The streamlined North Coast Limited was now on a fast, two-night-out schedule from Chicago to Seattle. (Another new train, the Mainstreeter, began service November 16, 1952, picking up many of the local stops that were dropped by the faster North Coast Limited schedule.) In the summer and fall of 1954, 10 dome coaches and 10 dome sleepers were delivered from the Budd Company in the new paint scheme. Northern Pacific had the only dome sleepers in the long haul, Midwest to Northwest run, beating rival Great Northern in the dome race. NP owned most of the new dome cars with some joint ownership by Burlington and the Spokane, Portland & Seattle Railway, which handled the train's Portland section from Pasco, Washington. On the beautiful new Vista-Dome

North Coast Limited, modern dome coaches allowed passengers spectacular views of 1,406 miles of river and 28 mountain ranges, particularly in Montana where the train followed the Lewis and Clark Trail. The popular "Traveller's Rest" lunch-counter-tavern cars (designed by Loewy and named after Lewis and Clark's favorite campsite in the Bitterroot Mountains) were built in the pioneer theme by Northern Pacific's Como Car Shops in St. Paul. The cars featured a wall-length diorama with maps and murals illustrating the remarkable Lewis and Clark Pacific Northwest Expedition in 1804. The observation-buffet-lounge sleeping car, complete with Monad emblem and illuminated tail-sign, was the perfect signature to a well-designed train. In 1955, uniformed stewardess-nurses were introduced to assist North Coast Limited passengers, and in 1959 the railroad started the modern, all-room Slumbercoach sleeping cars for economy-minded travelers.

Northern Pacific adopted the well-known slogan, "Main Street of the Northwest" in 1948, and the catchphrase was fitting, as NP served the larger cities in North Dakota, Montana, and Washington. Another Northern Pacific trademark was the semaphore signals along the Montana mainline. NP's company photographer often posed the flagship North Coast Limited by the semaphores for publicity photos. At Livingston, Montana, passengers going to Yellowstone National Park transferred trains and traveled 54 miles south on the Park Branch to the park entrance at Gardiner, Montana. Beginning in the late 1890s, Wonderland guidebooks, produced annually by the Northern Pacific, featured articles and photographs of Yellowstone National Park, western scenery, and train travel. NP continued to promote the park in travel brochures, magazines, and public timetables, including the slogan, "Yellowstone Park Line."

The Northern Pacific built its railroad over the rugged Cascade Mountains in the Pacific Northwest. The route followed the Yakima River west from Pasco, Washington, climbing the 2.2 percent mountain grades east and west of Stampede Pass and pushing through the 1.8-mile Stampede Tunnel, which was completed in 1888. Other spectacular mountain crossings were in Montana Big Sky Country. Those included Bozeman Pass (5,557 feet above sea level) near Livingston, named after John Bozeman, a Montana trailblazer killed in 1867 by the Blackfeet Tribe, and Homestake Pass (6,356 feet) at Butte, where NP trains crossed the Continental Divide. Northern Pacific's toughest and most impressive mountain crossing was Mullan Pass west of Helena, with a ruling grade of 2.2 percent westbound and 1.4 percent eastbound. The last portion of the climb to Mullan Pass' 5,548-foot summit was in the tunnel bore, which provided a dramatic finish for trains working up-grade, as locomotives charged out of the tunnel billowing clouds of smoke.

Because of the difficult western topography Northern Pacific was an early advocate of large steam locomotives. The first group of 12 Class A 4-8-4 Northerns were named for the railroad and built by American Locomotive Company (Alco) in 1926. From 1934 to 1943, NP ordered 36 more 4-8-4s from

Baldwin Locomotive Works. The Northerns fronted the North Coast Limited between St. Paul, Minnesota, and Livingston, Montana (a distance of over 1,000 miles), one of the longest steam assignments in railroad history. Other NP steam engines included the 2-8-8-4 Yellowstones, named for the river parallel to NP's Yellowstone Division. The first Yellowstone was built by Alco in 1928, was 125 feet long, and weighed 559 tons.

Eventually, Baldwin Locomotive Works would build 11 more and they became known as the "World's Largest Steam Locomotives." The huge engines worked trains on the east end of the Yellowstone Division from Mandan, North Dakota, to Glendive, Montana, and in helper service on the steep Montana grades. From 1936 through 1944, Northern Pacific received a fleet of 47 4-6-6-4 Challenger locomotives from Alco. They were used on the mountainous terrain between Glendive, Montana, and Easton, Washington, but not in the Stampede Tunnel because of narrow clearance. Northern Pacific dieselized most of its locomotive fleet beginning in 1944 with the Electro-Motive Division (EMD) FT freight series. Electro-Motive three-unit sets of F3s were delivered in 1947 to power the North Coast Limited. EMD F7s were acquired in 1949, F9s in 1954, and finally the General Purpose (GP) freight series. Baldwin and Alco also contributed switch engines and road engines to the NP fleet. By January 1959, dieselization had ended the Northern Pacific steam era. NP continued to upgrade its physical plant and yards, including the $5 million electronic freight classification yard at Pasco,

Washington. For its centennial year in 1964, NP authorized $35 million in improvements for welded rail, centralized traffic control, 15 new diesel locomotives, and 900 freight cars. Northern Pacific President Robert McFarland commented about Northern Pacific's next 100 years in *Railway Age* magazine (June 1964): "Population growth, and development of industry and natural resources, should mean boom years for the Pacific Northwest and the Northern Pacific."

After 106 years of continuous freight and passenger service, the Northern Pacific Railway was merged along with Great Northern, Chicago, Burlington & Quincy, and Spokane, Portland & Seattle Railway into the Burlington Northern system on March 2, 1970. The passenger-friendly Northern Pacific is best remembered for its flagship Vista-Dome North Coast Limited with spectacular scenery from Chicago to Seattle and famously good meals like fresh salmon, baked apples, and the "Great Big" Baked Potato.

Today, Northern Pacific's former route from St. Paul, Minnesota, to Fargo, North Dakota, is on Burlington Northern Santa Fe (BNSF) Railway's Chicago-Seattle mainline, which also hosts Amtrak's daily *Empire Builder*. The former Spokane, Portland & Seattle Railway line from Pasco, Washington, to Portland remains busy with BNSF freight, and regional carrier Montana Rail Link operates trains on former Northern Pacific trackage from Billings, Montana, to Sandpoint, Idaho. So in the way Northern Pacific originally intended, the "Main Street of the Northwest" continues to prosper as a major freight corridor.

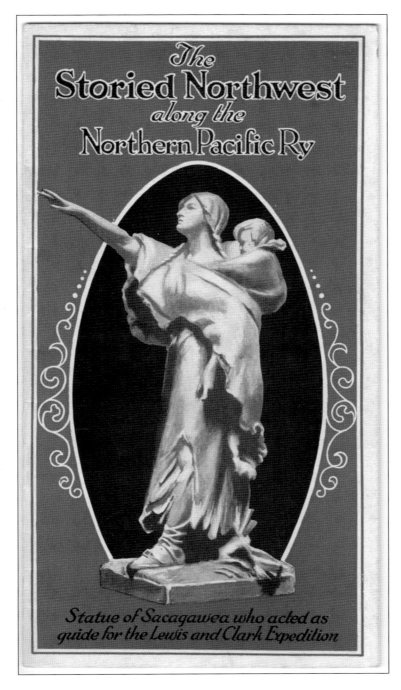

Statue of Sacagawea who acted as guide for the Lewis and Clark Expedition

Northern Pacific travel brochure featured Sacagawea, a 19-year-old Shoshone Indian mother who led explorers Lewis and Clark on their Pacific Northwest Expedition in 1804. *Author's collection*

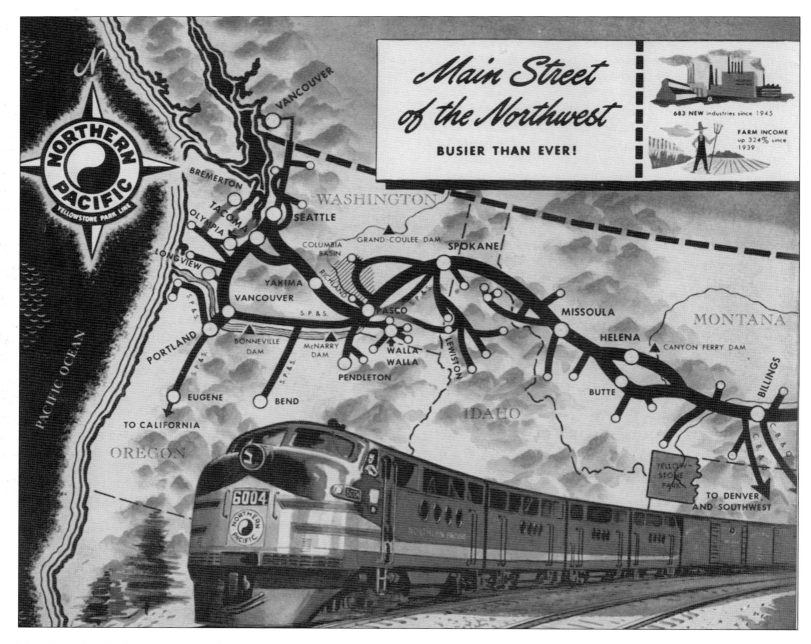

Northern Pacific "Main Street of the Northwest" route map from 1950 annual report. *Author's collection*

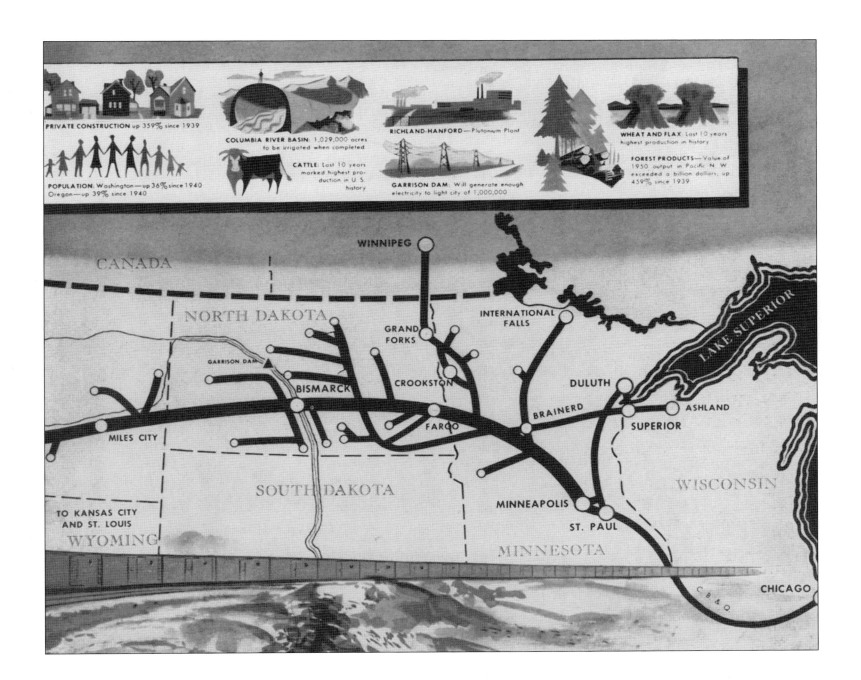

PRIVATE CONSTRUCTION up 359% since 1939

POPULATION: Washington—up 36% since 1940
Oregon—up 39% since 1940

COLUMBIA RIVER BASIN: 1,029,000 acres
to be irrigated when completed.

CATTLE: Last 10 years
marked highest pro-
duction in U.S.
history

RICHLAND-HANFORD—Plutonium Plant

GARRISON DAM: Will generate enough
electricity to light city of 1,000,000

WHEAT AND FLAX: Last 10 years
highest production in history

FOREST PRODUCTS—Value of
1950 output in Pacific N.W.
exceeded a billion dollars, up
459% since 1939

CANADA

NORTH DAKOTA

WINNIPEG

INTERNATIONAL
FALLS

LAKE SUPERIOR

GARRISON DAM

BISMARCK

GRAND
FORKS

CROOKSTON

DULUTH

ASHLAND

BRAINERD

SUPERIOR

MILES CITY

FARGO

SOUTH DAKOTA

WISCONSIN

TO KANSAS CITY
AND ST. LOUIS

WYOMING

MINNEAPOLIS

ST. PAUL

MINNESOTA

CHICAGO

C B & Q

9

The Pacific Northwest via North Coast Limited

Northern Pacific's flagship North Coast Limited was inaugurated April 29, 1900. North Coast Limited Train 1 departed St. Paul Union Depot July 30, 1934, on its journey to Seattle. Motive power for the heavyweight train was steam locomotive 2227 4-6-2 Pacific. *Denver Public Library—Western History Collection*

Northern Pacific passenger train led by steam locomotive 2656 4-8-4 Northern crossed the Missouri River near Bismarck, North Dakota, August 12, 1938. *Denver Public Library—Western History Collection*

Northern Pacific North Coast Limited Train 1 led by locomotive 2602 4-8-4 and eight-car train had a fine steam effect departing Billings, Montana, May 11, 1934. *Denver Public Library—Western History Collection*

Northern Pacific steam locomotive 1548 2-8-2 Mikado led Train 218, with connections at Livingston to Gardiner, Montana (54 miles), and Yellowstone National Park. *Denver Public Library—Western History Collection*

Northern Pacific steam locomotive 2650 4-8-4 Northern and the North Coast Limited near Montana's scenic Bozeman Pass (5,557 feet above sea level) July 12, 1946. *Ron Nixon photo, JM Gruber collection*

Before diesel locomotives the North Coast Limited ran in two sections, one for Pullman sleepers and one for coaches. Locomotive 2651 4-8-4 Northern had a powerful head of steam on November 12, 1946, location unknown. *Ron Nixon photo, JM Gruber collection*

Seattle's King Street Station was the western terminus for the North Coast Limited. Note the station's high clock tower (right) behind the train, August 22, 1943. *Ron Nixon photo, JM Gruber collection*

Northern Pacific travel brochure for the heavyweight North Coast Limited featured the classic NP Monad symbol and route map. *Author's collection*

The North Coast Limited was diesel powered in early 1947 when NP purchased its first passenger units: six 4,500-horsepower, A-B-B sets of Electro-Motive F3s (6500-6505). NP passenger Fs were painted in two-tone, dark olive green "Pine Tree" scheme with gold striping. The North Coast Limited departed St. Paul Union Depot, May 12, 1948. *Ron Nixon photo, JM Gruber collection*

World War II production restrictions slowed arrival of North Coast Limited streamlined cars. Cars arrived piecemeal between June 1946 and summer of 1948. North Coast Limited departed St. Paul Union Depot with landmark 1st National Bank building in the center background, June 2, 1951. *Ron Nixon photo, JM Gruber collection*

At its peak St. Paul Union Depot hosted passenger trains from nine railroads. Leaving St. Paul Union Depot for Minneapolis was Northern Pacific's North Coast Limited as the engineer waved to the photographer. *BNSF Archives*

North Coast Limited crossed the James J. Hill Stone Arch Bridge over the Mississippi River headed into Great Northern Station at Minneapolis on July 17, 1949. The Stone Arch Bridge was built in 1883. The bridge is 2,100 feet long, 76 feet high, and is highlighted by 15 semicircular stone arches. Today the bridge is a bike trail. *JM Gruber collection*

Manitoba Junction was situated between Detroit Lakes and Fargo, and was a junction for the Red River Branch to Winnipeg, Canada. The train (left) is westbound to Seattle and the train diverging (right) past the semaphore signal is en route to Winnipeg. *JM Gruber collection*

Fargo, North Dakota, was named for William Fargo, one of the founders of Wells-Fargo Express and a pioneer director of Northern Pacific Railway. NP Dormitory-Railway Post Office (RPO) car 426 was loaded with mail and express on June 10, 1952, at the Fargo depot. *JM Gruber collection*

North Coast Limited sleeper-observation car "Mountain Club" (1 compartment, 4 double bedrooms) at Livingston, Montana, June 9, 1949.
Ron Nixon photo, JM Gruber collection

Electro-Motive F3 6501 led the North Coast Limited in the Butte Mountains near Highview, Montana, circa 1949. *Ron Nixon photo, JM Gruber collection*

In a picture from the streamlined era, NP car attendants dressed in white coats waited for passengers to board the North Coast Limited at Missoula, Montana, circa 1952. Note the NP car department employee checking connections on sleeping car "Jamestown." *JM Gruber collection*

Where In The World does Northern Pacific find those helpful people who serve you on the Vista-Dome North Coast Limited? No train crew was ever more friendly, quicker to please, more genuinely interested in a passenger's comfort. There's something special about this magnificent train that goes beyond fine food, fine equipment, or even the route that takes you through some of America's finest scenery. It's a happy train with happy people . . . . . the kind that makes travel *fun* again!

NORTHERN   PACIFIC   RAILWAY
Route of the Vista-Dome North Coast Limited

Northern Pacific was proud of their train crews and on-board personnel, featuring them on dining car menus and public timetables. *Author's collection*

Electro-Motive F3 6503 led the North Coast Limited at Missoula, Montana, July 22, 1948. Missoula was Rocky Mountain Division Headquarters of the Northern Pacific Railway. *JM Gruber collection*

North Coast Limited sleeper-observation car "Montana Club" at Missoula, Montana, July 21, 1948. Missoula is a Salish Indian word meaning "Land of Sparkling Water." *Ron Nixon photo, JM Gruber collection*

North Coast Limited led by F3 6505 and FT (freight) 6007 waited for departure at Missoula, Montana, July 22, 1948. *Ron Nixon photo, JM Gruber collection*

Semaphore signals were used in many Northern Pacific publicity photographs. The semaphore signal number plates were significant and indicated milepost locations. Numbers ending with odd digits were westbound and those ending with even numbers (1246 in photo) were eastbound. North Coast Limited near Missoula, Montana, circa 1951. *Ron Nixon photo, JM Gruber collection*

From the end of World War II until late 1952, Northern Pacific mixed new streamlined cars with older heavyweight cars in the North Coast Limited consist. Schley, Montana, circa 1952. *Ron Nixon photo, JM Gruber collection*

Northern Pacific F3 6504 led the North Coast Limited around a scenic curve between Evaro and Arlee, Montana, in 1947. *Ron Nixon photo, JM Gruber collection*

Passengers aboard the North Coast Limited sleeper-observation car "Arlington Club" enjoyed the mountain views between Evaro and Arlee, Montana, July 15, 1949. *Ron Nixon photo, JM Gruber collection*

Electro-Motive F3 6504 at Arlee, Montana, July 22, 1948, led the two-tone, dark olive green North Coast Limited. *JM Gruber collection*

Northern Pacific travel brochure proclaimed "Pictures all the way" as the North Coast Limited traversed 1,406 miles of rivers on its Chicago-Seattle route. *Author's collection*

The Northern Pacific mainline was built near many scenic rivers and offered passengers beautiful vistas on the Pacific Northwest route. The North Coast Limited met another NP passenger train at Knowles, Montana, April 11, 1951. *Ron Nixon photo, JM Gruber collection*

Paradise, Montana, was a water station for Northern Pacific steam locomotives before they climbed the Bitterroot Range into Idaho. Note the water and coal facility behind the semaphore signal. On June 12, 1952, Electro-Motive F3 6503 and North Coast Limited approached the automatic block signal at Paradise, Montana. *JM Gruber collection*

On August 12, 1949, Electro-Motive F3 6506 was leading the semi-streamlined North Coast Limited with heavyweight car at Paradise, Montana. *Ron Nixon photo, JM Gruber collection*

Northern Pacific steam locomotive 5145 4-6-6-4 Challenger with freight train met NP passenger train in Idaho, circa 1949. *Ron Nixon photo, JM Gruber collection*

The North Coast Limited split the semaphore signals near Clark Fork, Idaho, where the Missoula and Flathead Rivers join to form the beautiful Clark Fork of the Columbia River, named after Capt. William Clark of the Lewis and Clark Expedition. *Ron Nixon photo, JM Gruber collection*

Northern Pacific passenger train with Electro-Motive F3 6508 stopped to board passengers, date and location unknown. *JM Gruber collection*

North Coast Limited sleeper-observation car "Spokane Club" at Seattle's King Street Station. *Ron Nixon photo, JM Gruber collection*

Postcard of Seattle's King Street Station for Northern Pacific-Great Northern trains and Union Station (right) for Union Pacific-Milwaukee Road trains. *Author's collection*

Railroad Terminals, Northern Pacific — Great Northern — Chicago Milwaukee, St. Paul, and Pacific and Union Pacific, Seattle, Washington   1536

Vista-Dome North Coast Limited and Mainstreeter

Northern Pacific Railway passenger ticket and folder for Vista-Dome North Coast Limited. *Author's collection*

YOU'LL LIKE THE FASTER NORTH COAST LIMITED

NEW SCHEDULE
—NORTH COAST LIMITED

WESTBOUND

Lv	Chicago	11:30 am
	St. Paul	6:30 pm
	Minneapolis	7:00 pm
	Fargo	11:25 pm
	Bismarck	2:49 am
Ar	Glendive	5:57 am
	Miles City	7:29 am
	Forsyth	8:27 am
	Billings	10:23 am
	Bozeman	1:25 pm
	Livingston	12:30 pm
	Helena	4:05 pm
	Butte	3:58 pm
	Missoula	6:20 pm
	Spokane	10:45 pm
	Yakima	3:30 am
	Portland	7:30 am
	Tacoma	8:00 am
	Seattle	8:00 am

EASTBOUND

Lv	Seattle	1:15 pm
	Tacoma	12:55 pm
	Portland	3:00 pm
	Yakima	5:50 pm
	Spokane	10:30 pm
	Missoula	5:00 am
	Butte	7:20 am
	Bozeman	10:02 am
	Helena	7:10 am
	Livingston	10:51 am
	Billings	12:58 pm
	Forsyth	2:49 pm
	Miles City	3:42 pm
	Glendive	5:15 pm
	Bismarck	10:19 pm
	Fargo	1:47 am
Ar	Minneapolis	6:10 am
	St. Paul	6:40 am
	Chicago	1:45 pm

...for comfortable travel West

You'll gain extra hours for vacation fun as you relax aboard Northern Pacific's streamlined North Coast Limited—now 12 hours faster between Chicago and the North Pacific Coast. You'll enjoy real western hospitality, including meals that have made NP famous for years. You'll make convenient connections too—at Portland with California streamliners, at Chicago with Eastern and Southern "name" trains.

A second transcontinental train, "The Mainstreeter", also offers daily service to western travelers. For fares and schedules, for information about Pacific Northwest vacations, Yellowstone, Dude Ranches or Alaska Cruises —see your favorite travel or ticket agent, or write . . .

G. W. RODINE, *Passenger Traffic Manager*
701 Northern Pacific Railway, St. Paul 1, Minn.

NORTHERN PACIFIC RAILWAY — *Main Street of the Northwest*

"You'll Like The Faster North Coast Limited," proclaimed the November 15, 1952, schedule change. The updated North Coast Limited was assigned new train numbers (25 westbound and 26 eastbound) with two overnights on the Chicago-Seattle route. *Author's collection*

Electro-Motive Division advertisement for F9 passenger locomotives to power the North Coast Limited and Mainstreeter. *Author's collection*

Great new line of

GENERAL MOTORS LOCOMOTIVES

7000

7001

11 NEW 1750-HORSEPOWER F9 UNITS TO NORTHERN PACIFIC

These new and more powerful General Motors locomotives are being added to the passenger pool handling the North Coast Limited and the Mainstreeter—two of the more than 200 famous name trains powered by General Motors Diesel locomotives. Delivery of these latest units brings the fleet of General Motors Diesel locomotives now serving the Northern Pacific to a total of 224.

General Motors Diesel locomotives outnumber all others on American railroads because twenty years' experience proves they operate on more dependable schedules—cost less to operate and maintain—*pay for themselves faster than any others!*

THE BEST LOCOMOTIVES ARE EVEN BETTER TODAY!

ELECTRO-MOTIVE DIVISION · GENERAL MOTORS

GENERAL MOTORS
LOCO.MOTIVES

La Grange, Illinois · Home of the Diesel Locomotive · In Canada: GENERAL MOTORS DIESEL, LTD., London, Ontario

In 1954, Electro-Motive replaced the F7 with more powerful F9 locomotives rated at 1,750 horsepower. Northern Pacific locomotive F9 6705A was photographed in the Raymond Loewy-designed two-tone green with white band at Bozeman, Montana, November 8, 1966. *JM Gruber collection*

Northern Pacific public timetable (April 5, 1954) previewed the new Vista-Dome coaches and sleepers built by the Budd Company, scheduled for delivery in late summer 1954. This put Northern Pacific one step ahead of rival Great Northern in dome-sleeping cars. *Author's collection*

NEW *Vista-Domes* ARE COMING !

Late this summer, a fleet of new Vista-Dome coaches and sleeping cars will go in service on the *faster* North Coast Limited between Chicago and the North Pacific Coast. Northern Pacific's scenic mountain route will be more spectacular than ever when viewed from the dome of one of these luxurious new cars. There will be two Dome coaches and two Dome sleeping cars on each North Coast Limited when all cars are in service. Each dome seats 24 passengers.

NORTHERN PACIFIC RAILWAY
Route of the *faster* NORTH COAST LIMITED

Form 5111   Made in U. S. A.   Corrected to April 5. 1954.

In a classic Northern Pacific company photo the Vista-Dome North Coast Limited emerged from Jefferson Canyon, east of the Continental Divide in Montana. *Author's collection*

Westbound Train 25, Vista-Dome North Coast Limited arrived at Billings, Montana, with 13 cars on July 2, 1967. *Denver Public Library—Western History Collection*

Northern Pacific locomotives and North Coast Limited were ready to depart Seattle, circa 1950s. Note the vintage automobiles in the photo. *Denver Public Library—Western History Collection*

Sue the steward- ess says:

"Plan your next trip on Northern Pacific's Vista-Dome North Coast Limited. It's the train that makes travel fun again.

"I'll be aboard to welcome you, and the friendly crew on the North Coast Limited will make your trip a most pleasant travel adventure.

"Treat yourself to the finest in travel . . . go Northern Pacific."

The Vista-Dome NORTH COAST LIMITED

Chicago · Twin Cities · Billings · Spokane · Portland · Seattle

A CHOICE OF ACCOMMODATIONS

RECLINING SEAT COACH • SLUMBERCOACH • PULLMAN

FOR
- TICKETS
- INFORMATION
- RESERVATIONS

Call or write your nearest Northern Pacific Representative

or

Passenger Traffic Manager
Northern Pacific Railway Company
St. Paul, Minn. 55101

FORM 6976 3-68 14

 MAIN STREET OF THE NORTHWEST

North Coast Limited stewardess-nurse service was inaugurated June 1955. "Sue the Stewardess" was featured in advertisements and Northern Pacific travel brochures. *Author's collection*

"Traveller's Rest," for which this de luxe car was named, was a favorite campsite of explorers Lewis and Clark

Passengers aboard the North Coast Limited could write home on complimentary postcards. One postcard showed the "Traveller's Rest" lounge car with wall-to-ceiling, spot lit diorama of the Lewis and Clark Expedition described by NP stewardess-nurse. *Author's collection*

The *Vista-Dome* North Coast Limited opens a new panorama of scenic beauty to travelers in the Northern Pacific West

"Great Big" Baked Potato

This exclusive Northern Pacific dish and many others make meal time an experience to be anticipated with utmost pleasure on the

Air-Conditioned

NORTH COAST LIMITED

H. C. HASBERG
Traveling Passenger Agent
NORTHERN PACIFIC RAILWAY
St. Paul, Minn.

The "Great Big" Baked Potato helped promote Northern Pacific dining cars and their slogan, "Famously good meals."

North Coast Limited drink coaster. *Author's collection*

60

LUNCHEON

Served from 12 NOON to 2:30 P.M.

SALAD SUGGESTION $1.95

Peach or Pear and Cottage Cheese Salad
(N. P. dressing)

Buttered Toast   Ry-Krisp

Orange Sherbet

Coffee   Tea (hot or iced)   Milk

LUNCHEON SUGGESTION $2.40

Broiled Fresh Fish (in season)

or

Spaghetti and Meat Balls, Italian Style

Choice ⎰ Oven Brown Potatoes
of   ⎰ Garden Peas
Two   ⎱ Vegetable Salad

Luncheon roll and butter

Coffee   Tea (hot or iced)   Milk
(No substitutions please)

Freshly Baked Pie—Ice Cream or Sherbet—25¢
additional with above suggestions

A LA CARTE

APPETIZERS

Chef's soup, cup, crackers	.40
Chef's soup, tureen, crackers	.60
Fruit cocktail	.60
Crabmeat or shrimp cocktail	$1.00

VEGETABLES

Garden peas	.35
Whole kernel corn	.35
Hashed-browned or American fried potatoes	.45

BREADS

Assorted Breads .25		Hol-Ry .25
Hot Rolls .25		Ry-Krisp .25

BEVERAGES

Buttermilk .25	Milk .25	Coffee (pot) .30
Instant Sanka Coffee (pot) .30		Tea (pot) .30
Creamy hot chocolate (pot)		.35

SANDWICHES

Grilled Cheese, Pickle	.70
Ground Beefburger 6-oz.	.85
Sugar cured baked ham, tomato slices	.95
Cold roast beef, radishes	.95
Ham and egg, potato chips	$1.20
Special club house, olives, potato chips	$1.70
Broiled 8-oz. Tenderloin Steak, on toast	$2.85

SALADS

Lettuce and tomato	.95
Combination (crisp lettuce, ripe tomato, radishes, celery, peas, green beans, cucumber, green pepper)	$1.45
Chicken salad, Hard boiled egg	$1.45
Seafood (crab, lobster, shrimp, sardines)	$1.75

Choice of: N.P. Dressing, 1000 Island,
French, Blue Cheese, Mayonnaise
(Crackers and butter served with salads)

DESSERTS

Freshly baked pie .25		Pie A La Mode .60
French vanilla ice cream .40		Sherbet .40
Fruited Jello, whipped topping		.40
Elberta peaches or Bartlett pears in syrup		
		(sugar wafer) .45

Waiters are instructed not to take oral orders.

This Car Is Open For Beverage Service Throughout The Day, Subject To State And Federal Regulations

Passengers On Special Diet Are Invited To Make Known Their Requirements To The Steward

Dietetic Foods and Low Calorie Syrup Available

ROOM SERVICE
A charge of 50¢ per person will be made for food service outside the dining car. This service is subject to delay when dining car is busy.

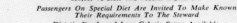

ROUTE OF THE *Vista-Dome* NORTH COAST LIMITED

Steward will provide small traveler's menu for children

W. F. PAAR	F. G. SCOTT
Superintendent Dining Car Department	Passenger Traffic Manager
8235-NCL	C-3-67

Vista-Dome North Coast Limited luncheon menu, March 1967. *Author's collection*

Vista-Dome North Coast Limited with CB&Q motive power was eastbound at Oregon, Illinois, October 11, 1955. *D. Christensen photo, Bill Raia collection*

North Coast Limited observation car 394 crossed the CB&Q-Milwaukee Road interlocking at Savanna, Illinois, on April 19, 1964. *Bill Raia collection*

Second to the famed North Coast Limited was the Mainstreeter, inaugurated November 16, 1952. The Mainstreeter was assigned the old North Coast Limited Train numbers 1 and 2, including many of the local passenger stops enroute. *Author's collection*

Schedule of THE MAINSTREETER

WESTBOUND Read Down TRAIN NO. 1			EASTBOUND Read Up TRAIN NO. 2
11:10 pm	Lv. Chicago *CB&Q*	Ar.	7:55 am
8:40 am	Lv. St. Paul N.P.Ry.	Ar.	10:30 pm
9:15 am	Lv. Minneapolis	Ar.	9:57 pm
10:32 am	Lv. St. Cloud	Ar.	8:34 pm
11:05 am	Lv. Little Falls	Ar.	7:55 pm
7:25 am	Lv. Duluth	Ar.	11:10 pm
7:39 am	Lv. Superior	Ar.	10:49 pm
10:29 am	Lv. Brainerd	Ar.	8:02 pm
11:51 am	Lv. Staples	Ar.	7:10 pm
2:30 pm	Lv. Fargo	Ar.	4:30 pm
3:26 pm	Lv. Valley City	Ar.	3:26 pm
4:27 pm	Lv. Jamestown	Ar.	2:35 pm
6:30 pm	Lv. Bismarck	Ar.	12:48 pm
6:47 pm	Ar. Mandan (C.S.T.)	Lv.	12:38 pm
5:57 pm	Lv. Mandan (M.S.T.)	Ar.	11:28 am
8:10 pm	Lv. Dickinson	Ar.	9:23 am
10:28 pm	Ar. Glendive	Lv.	7:16 am
12:35 am	Ar. Miles City	Lv.	5:00 am
1:43 am	Ar. Forsyth	Lv.	3:53 am
3:58 am	Ar. Billings	Lv.	1:48 am
7:00 am	Ar. Livingston	Lv.	11:08 pm
8:27 am	Ar. Bozeman	Lv.	9:45 pm
11:15 am	Ar. Helena	Lv.	7:00 pm
11:30 am	Ar. Butte	Lv.	6:35 pm
3:20 pm	Ar. Missoula	Lv.	3:10 pm
5:30 pm	Ar. Paradise (M.S.T.)	Lv.	1:01 pm
4:40 pm	Lv. Paradise (P.S.T.)	Ar.	11:56 am
8:25 pm	Ar. Spokane	Lv.	8:18 am
6:00 am	Ar. Portland SP&S	Lv.	9:45 pm
12:01 am	Ar. Pasco	Lv.	4:50 am
2:25 am	Ar. Yakima	Lv.	2:25 am
3:47 am	Ar. Ellensburg	Lv.	1:11 am
4:21 am	Ar. Cle Elum	Lv.	12:31 am
7:30 am	Ar. Tacoma	Lv.	9:10 pm
7:40 am	Ar. Seattle	Lv.	9:35 pm

CALIFORNIA CONNECTIONS (Southern Pacific Ry.)

#19	#11	#9		#20	#10	#12
10:15 pm	4:45 pm	7:45 am	Lv. Portland Ar.	7:25 pm	11:25 pm	8:20 am
7:40 pm	8:35 am	10:55 pm	Ar. Oakland Lv.	8:05 pm	7:55 pm	4:35 pm
8:20 pm	9:15 am	11:30 pm	Ar. San Fran. Lv.	7:30 pm	7:30 am	4:00 pm
10:50 am	7:00 pm	10:50 am	Ar. Los A. Lv.	6:25 am	6:05 pm	6:25 am

Regular equipment on *The Mainstreeter* includes a diner, serving "famously good" NP meals; lightweight, streamlined sleeping cars with roomettes, duplex roomettes, bedrooms and compartments; deluxe coaches with adjustable seats and foot rests, and the luxurious new Holiday Lounge Car described in this folder.

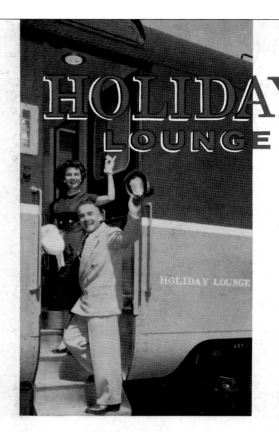

NEW LUXURY CAR
on the

MAINSTREETER

CHICAGO . . . ST. PAUL . . . MINNEAPOLIS . . . SPOKANE
PORTLAND . . . TACOMA . . . SEATTLE

SCENIC ROUTE OF

THE MAINSTREETER
AND THE VISTA-DOME

NORTH COAST LIMITED

NORTHERN PACIFIC RAILWAY—ST. PAUL 1, MINN.

F6933 Printed in U.S.A. 9/56

The Mississippi River in the foreground and Great Northern Minneapolis Station (upper right) were the setting for the arrival of what is most likely the Mainstreeter. No date or train name. *Bob's photo*

Observation car "Yakima River" on the Mainstreeter at Missoula, Montana, March 15, 1962. *Jim Scribbins photo, Bill Raia collection*

In 1903, Lima Locomotive Works built Shay 0-6-0 locomotives for the Washington State logging industry and eventually Northern Pacific acquired three of them. NP locomotive 9 at Tacoma, Washington, April 1957. *Bruce Meyer photo*

Northern Pacific steam locomotive 1065 (six wheel switcher) Class L9 built by Manchester Locomotive Works in 1907 at Duluth, Minnesota, August 14, 1953. *JM Gruber collection*

Northern Pacific steam locomotive 2450 2-6-2 Prairie Class T at St. Paul, Minnesota, September 1, 1946. *JM Gruber collection*

The Mikado Class W steam locomotives were the largest group of one class and worked in all types of Northern Pacific train service. Locomotive 1515 2-8-2 Mikado Class W, at St. Paul, Minnesota, August 27, 1937. *JM Gruber collection*

Northern Pacific steam locomotive 1616 2-8-2 Mikado Class W at Yakima, Washington, September 12, 1954. *JM Gruber collection*

Northern Pacific public timetable (June 3, 1945) back cover featured Fact or Fiction trivia quiz. *Author's collection*

Northern Pacific steam locomotive 2683 4-8-4 Northern Class A5 built by Baldwin Locomotive Works in 1943, at Staples, Minnesota, September 6, 1955. The "Northerns" were billed as the longest locomotives in the American Northwest and powered NP passenger trains. *JM Gruber collection*

Northern Pacific steam locomotive 4025 2-8-8-2 Articulated Class Z3 built by American Locomotive Company in 1920. The big locomotives pulled NP freights and worked helper service at Livingston and Bozeman, Montana. Date and location unknown. *JM Gruber collection*

In 1928, Northern Pacific introduced the 2-8-8-4 Articulated Yellowstone, named for the river parallel to NP's Yellowstone Division. Built by American Locomotive Company, the massive locomotives worked full tonnage freight trains from Mandan, North Dakota, to Glendive, Montana, until 1944. Yellowstone 5003 at Glendive, Montana, date unknown. *JM Gruber collection*

Between 1936 and 1944 Northern Pacific received a fleet of 47 4-6-6-4 Class Z6 Challenger locomotives from American Locomotive Company. The Challengers hauled trains on the mountainous terrain between Glendive, Montana, and Easton, Washington. Challenger 5100 at Livingston, Montana, July 7, 1955. *JM Gruber collection*

Northern Pacific 4-6-6-4 Challenger steam locomotive 5122 with tank cars at Missoula, Montana, May 27, 1946. *Ron Nixon photo, JM Gruber collection*

In 1939, Electro-Motive introduced the four-unit FT (freight) set comprised of two A-unit cabs and two B-unit cabless booster units in A-B-B-A configuration. The FTs had a 5,400-horsepower rating and sported a streamlined look with rounded "Bull Dog" nose. NP locomotive 5409D at Missoula, Montana, June 14, 1964. *JM Gruber collection*

The Electro-Motive F3 premiered in 1946 as a powerful 6,000-horsepower, 4-unit set coupled in A-B configurations. Unlike the FT sets, the F3s gave the railroad more flexibility in locomotive assignments. *EMD photo, Author's collection*

Electro-Motive F3 6000D, three-unit A-B-B set was used in freight pool service. Note the "Main Street of the Northwest" slogan on the B-units, shown here at Savanna, Illinois, May 18, 1966. *JM Gruber collection*

In 1949, Electro-Motive introduced its popular F7 locomotive. The F7 had improved traction motor design and new fuel injection system that allowed the locomotive to burn cheaper grades of fuel. The F7 was one of Electro-Motive's best selling models with 3,849 units sold to North American railroads. Northern Pacific F7 6015A at Schiller Park, Illinois, April 30, 1969. *Bill Raia photo, JM Gruber collection*

Northern Pacific F7 6020D at Livingston, Montana, June 10, 1964. *JM Gruber collection*

In 1941, American Locomotive Company introduced the RS-1 (road switcher), six-cylinder engine rated at 1,000 horsepower. The RS-1 was intended for yard switching and light road assignments. RS-1 801 at Duluth, Minnesota, July 27, 1967. *JM Gruber collection*

American Locomotive Company improved the road switcher models in the 1950s. The RS-3 had increased horsepower and other diesel-mechanical improvements. RS-3 switch engines were set to operate long-hood forward, but, due to smoky diesel exhaust, crews preferred short-hood forward. RS-3 853 at Minneapolis, Minnesota, April 1963. *T. Strauss photo, Bill Raia collection*

Northern Pacific RS-3 855 derailed at Rice's Point Yard in Duluth, Minnesota, July 27, 1961. *CF Sager photo, John Pedersen collection*

Northern Pacific Alco RS-11 905 at Superior, Wisconsin, July 27, 1967. *JM Gruber collection*

Northern Pacific Alco RS-11 907 with taconite train at Superior, Wisconsin, July 27, 1967. *JM Gruber collection*

From 1953 to 1963, Electro-Motive built more than 4,200 GP9s for North American railroads. NP favored the new locomotive and purchased over 150 GP9s between 1954 and 1958. GP9 317 at Minneapolis, Minnesota, April 1960. *Bill Raia collection*

Overhead view of GP9 373 at Northern Pacific's Minneapolis yard. The highly successful GP9 locomotive offered improved performance in cold Minnesota winters. Photographed in May 1960. *T. Strauss photo, Bill Raia collection*

General Electric built the U28C locomotive based on the popular U25C six-axle series. The "U" signified "Universal" and was designed as heavy road power, typically operated in sets of three or four. Here is U28C 2806, date and location unknown. *JM Gruber collection*

General Electric U33C locomotives were designed with 3,300 horsepower for mainline freight service, like U33C 3308 at Cicero, Illinois, June 4, 1970. *JM Gruber collection*

Electro-Motive SD45. The "SD" denoted "Special Duty" and was a turbo-charged, high 3,600-horsepower, six-axle locomotive built in the late 1960s. NP used the SD45s to haul heavy freight trains over the steep Montana mountain grades. Shown is SD45 3603 at Laurel, Montana, September 8, 1968. *JM Gruber collection*

Northern Pacific SD45 3621 without its NP nose herald at Cicero, Illinois, June 28, 1970. *JM Gruber collection*

Northern Pacific SW9 118 switch engine at Bayport, Minnesota, July 24, 1967. *JM Gruber collection*

Northern Pacific SW1200 151 switch engine at St. Paul, Minnesota, July 24, 1967. *JM Gruber collection*

In the 1930s many NP short-haul steam-powered passenger trains were replaced by gas-electric motorcars. The gas-electric motorcar contained the Railway Post Office (RPO) compartment behind the engine room, space for baggage and freight (milk cans), and passenger seating at the rear. NP motorcar B-13 at Valley City, North Dakota. *JM Gruber collection*

Northern Pacific motorcar B-18 served several years on the Centralia to South Bend turn. B-18 was also used in Montana passenger service and finished its career in Duluth and Staples, Minnesota. *Bill Raia collection*

Northern Pacific motorcar B-18 at Union Depot in Duluth, Minnesota, September 22, 1963. Duluth was Lake Superior Division Headquarters of the Northern Pacific. *CF Sager photo, John Pedersen collection*

In 1949, the Budd Company introduced its modern Rail Diesel Car-RDC1 with twin under-floor engines. NP purchased RDC B-40 and B-41 in March 1955 and September 1956, respectively. Both RDC cars operated as Trains 57 and 58 between Duluth-Superior and Staples, Minnesota. RDC B-41 at Staples, Minnesota, date unknown. *JM Gruber collection*

The Budd-built RDC cars were well liked by passengers and included modern interiors with exterior stainless steel and fluted sides, similar to Burlington Zephyrs. RDC B-42 at Duluth, Minnesota, July 27, 1967. *O. Leander photo, Bill Raia collection*

Northern Pacific Freight cars, Maintenance-of-way and Cabooses

America's secret weapon is locked in this car

Its name is *capacity*.

We have plenty of it. You'll find it both in the brand new NP car of 61 tons load limit shown above and in every other freight car in operation today.

But as a weapon to win this war, freight car capacity is useless unless it is rolling swiftly to its destination on rails. It has been estimated that American railroads can, without putting in service a single new car, add 10% to their rolling stock tomorrow *simply by keeping cars fully loaded and by keeping them on the move.* Not on spurs, not on sidings. Not "waiting till tomorrow" to unload or load.

Northern Pacific pledges every effort to help . . . to spot cars promptly, to remove empties or loaded cars punctually.

NP rails are carrying lots of extra trains these days. With the help of shippers and receivers, they can carry many more. Let's use our secret weapon to the full!

NORTHERN PACIFIC RAILWAY—*"Main Street of the Northwest"*

Northern Pacific public timetable (June 19, 1942) advertisement for freight car capacity. *Author's collection*

Northern Pacific double-door, 50-foot steel boxcar 2267 featured large NP decals and passenger slogan, "Route of the Vista-Dome North Coast Limited." Here at Zanesville, Ohio, May 18, 1962. *JM Gruber collection*

Northern Pacific 40-foot boxcar 9792 proudly displayed the motto, "Main Street of the Northwest," here at Zanesville, Ohio, December 10, 1956. *JM Gruber collection*

Northern Pacific 3-bay center flow covered hopper car 76366 at Zanesville, Ohio. *JM Gruber collection*

Northern Pacific open hopper car 73673 at Zanesville, Ohio. *JM Gruber collection*

Northern Pacific refrigerator car 91483 at Milwaukee, Wisconsin, September 25, 1968. *JM Gruber collection*

Northern Pacific gondola car 53342 with load at Milwaukee, Wisconsin, March 4, 1968. *JM Gruber collection*

Brainerd, Minnesota, is located at the geographical center of Minnesota and was founded in 1870, when Northern Pacific's survey determined that its Mississippi River crossing should be located at Brainerd. Northern Pacific railroad shops and yards dominated the city for many years. Northern Pacific Brainerd car shops, photographed on September 3, 1956. *Bruce Meyer photo*

Northern Pacific public timetable (October 1945) back cover featured "Massportation" advertisement for NP track crew replacing rail along the "Main Street of the Northwest." *Author's collection*

Northern Pacific shops built the weed burner car used to keep mainline and branch lines clear. Here at Mandan, North Dakota, July 26, 1934. *Denver Public Library—Western History Collection*

Northern Pacific rail detector car B-103 at Duluth, Minnesota, November 5, 1966. *CF Sager photo, John Pedersen collection*

The Russell Car & Snow Plow Company of Ridgeway, Pennsylvania, built wedge-type Russell snow plows for the railroads until the early 1950s. Most plows were un-powered and operated in heavy snow service with pusher locomotives. NP Russell Snow Plow 22. *Denver Public Library—Western History Collection*

Spreader cars were used by Maintenance-of-way crews and considered "dual purpose" pieces of equipment used for ballast spreading and snow removal. Most Spreaders were un-powered and assisted by pusher locomotives. NP Spreader car 447 at Superior, Wisconsin, August 28, 1969. *O. Leander photo, Bill Raia collection*

Northern Pacific-Soo Line combined freight house in Ashland, Wisconsin. *CF Sager photo, John Pedersen collection*

Northern Pacific wood caboose 10744 coupled to a freight train, St. Paul, Minnesota, May 31, 1971. *Bill Raia collection*

Northern Pacific bay-window caboose 1530 at Livingston, Montana, August 19, 1968. *L. Hestman photo, Bill Raia collection*

Northern Pacific all-steel, cupola caboose 10102 with "Main Street of the Northwest" slogan. Date and location unknown. *JM Gruber collection*

Observation car tail-sign for Northern Pacific Railway North Coast Limited. *Doug Wornom collection*

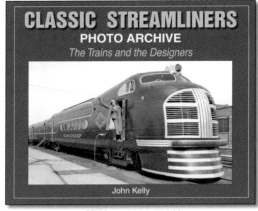
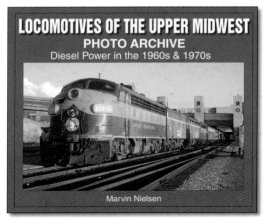
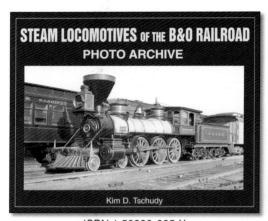
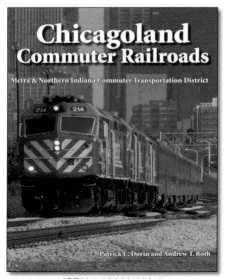
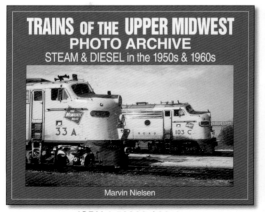